compiled by John Vince

illustrated by Christine Jopling

The Countryman

First published in Great Britain 2010 by Countryman Publishing
an imprint of
Country Publications Ltd
The Water Mill, Broughton Hall
Skipton, North Yorkshire BD23 3AG

ISBN 978-1-85568-277-1

Printed by in China by Latitude Press Ltd.

Introduction

This Little Book of country sayings and proverbs represents one feature of language that is so frequently used that it is scarcely noticed in everyday conversation: concise ideas are more easily remembered.

The ability of people to compress a good deal of meaning into a very small space has a long pedigree. In these pages you will find examples that are probably very old, but their meaning still has an impact on the listener. Proverbs go straight to the point and no word is wasted.

Fashions change in language, and some of our examples may have been forgotten in the turbulence of modern-day forms of speech.

Many of the sayings here have parallels in other countries.

These sayings, proverbs and old wives' tales are treasures to be valued.

John Vince

Weather

The farther the sight,
The nearer the rain.

When there is a thunderstorm
cover up all your mirrors.

Hampshire, 1880

Rain on Good Friday,
And wet Easter Day,
Plenty of grass
But little good hay.

When the wind is in the North
the skilful fisherman goes not forth;
When the wind is in the South
it blows the bait in the fish's mouth;
When the wind is in the East
they won't bite in the least;
When the wind is in the West
the fish bite best.

A dry May and a dripping June
Brings all things into tune.

saying from Bedfordshire

When the moon is at the full,
Mushrooms you may freely pull;
But when the moon is on the wane,
Wait, ere you think to pluck again.

The farmer should have
at Candlemas Day
Half his straw
and half his hay.

(Candlemas falls on 2nd February)

If Candlemas Day be fair and bright,
Winter will have another flight:
But if Candlemas Day be clouds and rain,
Winter is gone and will not come again.

If Candlemas day be mild and gay,
Go saddle your horses, and buy them hay;
But if Candlemas Day be stormy and black,
It carries the winter away on its back.

On St Joseph's Day,
Fling the warming pan away.

(St Joseph's Day falls on 19th March)

When gnats dance in February,
The husbandman becomes a beggar.

A January spring
Is worth nothing.

*(an unseasonably mild start to the year
is not good for crops)*

If you see grass in January
Lock your grain in your granary.

*(a variation on the sentiments
expressed on the opposite page)*

Observe the way the hedgehog builds
her nest,
To front the north or south or east or west:
For if 'tis true that common people say,
The wind will blow the quite contrary way;
If by some secret art the hedgehogs know,
So long before, which way the winds
will blow,
She has an art to which many a
person lacks,
That thinks himself fit to make almanacs.

Poor Robin's Almanac (1733)

Onion skin very thin,
Mild winter coming in;
Onion skin thick and tough,
Coming winter cold and rough.

from Five Hundred Points of Good Husbandry *by Thomas Tusser (1524-80)*

A rainbow at night
Is the shepherd's delight.
A rainbow in the morning
Is the shepherd's warning.

(the shepherd's rule)

Evening grey and morning red,
Sends the shepherd wet to bed.
Evening red and morning grey,
Is the sign of a very fine day.

On Thursday at three
Look out and you'll see
What Friday will be.

The north wind blows for energy,
The east wind stirs men's temper,
The west wind blows for friendship,
And the south wind for love.

Ireland

When sheep rise early to feed,
rain is ahead.

A ring round the moon
It will rain very soon.

When cows lie down in a field before eleven o'clock it will rain before night.

When old cats play
it means rain.

It is bad luck to point to a rainbow.

Herefordshire

Home & Garden

Hawthorn bloom and elder flowers
Will fill a house with evil powers.

Warwickshire
(hawthorn and elder should not
be brought indoors)

The fair maid, who, the first of May,
Goes to the fields at break of day,
And washes in dew from the
hawthorn tree,
Will ever after handsome be.

Many eyes pass through a meadow
but few notice the flowers.

(cultivate the practice of observation)

One day is worth two tomorrows.

(a variant on the Latin proverb
Carpe diem *or 'seize the day')*

If apples bloom in March
In vain for them you'll search;
If apples bloom in April
Why then they'll be plentiful;
If apples bloom in May
You may eat them night and day.

(a reminder that spring frosts were often the greatest danger to apple crops)

Who sets an apple tree
May live to see it end;
Who sets a pear tree
May set it for a friend.

(Old pear varieties were particularly slow growing and it was many years before they started to bear fruit)

It is unlucky for a clock to stand facing the fire.

S O Addy, 1895

It is unlucky to have an odd number
of people in a kitchen.

traditional, recorded in 1797

If a person rising from a table overturns the chair it shows that they have been speaking untruths.

A Napier, 1879

Never pass a chair across a table
as it will foretell a row.

Hunger will break through stone walls,
or anything but Suffolk cheese.

*(a calumny upon the cheese makers
of the county)*

The cat would eat fish
And would not wet her feet,
They must hunger in frost
That will not work in heat.

*(you must work in demanding conditions
if you are to reap a just reward)*

Friday's hair and Sunday's horn
Goes to the Devil on Monday morn.

Ray, Proverbs *(1678)*
(cutting hair or nails on a Friday
was considered bad luck)

Those who bathe in May
Will soon be laid in clay;
They who bathe in June
Will sing another tune.

*(bathing during the colder months
was not thought to be a good thing
in Georgian times)*

If a teapot lid is left off,
it denotes the coming of a stranger.

Gentleman's Magazine, *1855*

Never cut a mince pie
because you cut your luck.

Yorkshire

Never burn elder wood indoors as it
may cause a death in the house.

traditional

By hook and by crook.

(an expression that reminds us of the peasants' right on a mediaeval manor to collect wood for fuel; the hook was for cutting green wood and the crook for breaking off the dead branches)

He that makes himself an ass must not mind if men ride him.

old proverb

If the Devil catch a man idle
he will set him to work.

Thomas Fuller, Gnomologia, Adagies and Proverbs *(1732)*

On a farm where there are geese,
the farmer's wife wears the britches.

(poultry are traditionally the responsibility of the farmer's wife, and geese are unpopular with farmers because of the amount of grass they consume)

Love thy neighbour,
but pull not down thy hedge.

If a man treads on the fire tongs
in the morning he need not go
fishing in the afternoon.

from 1809

Before setting out on a journey,
turn the fire tongs for luck.

Children pick up words
As pigeons gather peas,
And utter them again
As God shall please.

Thou art promising me the birds,
but I must catch them myself.

Isle of Man

Two women should not try to set the same fire as they will have a falling out.

(this is similar to the idea that you should not have two cooks in the same kitchen)

The withes (bands) used to bind the faggots used in a bread oven should never be burnt or the oven will not get hot.

A child born on New Year's Day
will be very lucky.

(the same belief is also attached to the first of the month or the day of a new moon)

Farming

One boy is a boy,
Two boys are half a boy,
Three boys are no boys at all.

Bert Sheffield, Buckinghamshire
(a bird-scaring rhyme on the theme of 'experience is better than youth': one boy will work without distraction; two boys will distract one another and half the work is lost; three boys will disrupt one another and no work will be done)

If your farm is manned with boys
and horsed with colts,
your food is all eaten
and your work undone.

(another reminder of the value of experience)

There are three ways of losing money:
Backing horses is the quickest,
Wine and women are the pleasantest,
But fattening bullocks is the surest.

(the winter fattening of cattle rarely brought a profit)

Cadows and crows,
Take care of your toes.
For here come my clappers
To knock you down back'uds.
Holla Ca-whoo, Ca-whoo!

Here comes a stone
To break your backbone.
Here come the farmer with his big gun
And you must fly and I must run.
Holla Ca-whoo, Ca-whoo!

bird-scaring rhyme

Baked meat is better than boiled.

(cattle fare better in a dry grazing season than a wet one)

In the spring, hair is worth more than meat.

(cattle which have spent the winter outdoors are more valuable than cattle which have been kept indoors)

Everyone has his own row to hoe.

East Anglia

God calls men when they are busy,
Satan when they are idle.

A full sack can bear a blow in the side, and never be worse for it.

(prosperous people can afford to listen to envious remarks)

Plant your 'taturs when you will,
They won't come up before April.

Wiltshire

The master's foot
is the best manure.

(the master's foot which had trodden all his acres allowed him to spot and destroy all the unwanted weeds; this habit was held to be as effective as good manure)

The presence of the master
is the profit of the field.

Plough deep while sluggards sleep
And you shall have corn to sell and keep.

(A variant of 'No pain without gain')

A farmer should live as though
he were going to die tomorrow,
But he should farm as though
he were going to live forever.

Nothing is less profitable
than to cultivate land to perfection.

(a translation of Pliny the Elder's
Nihil minus expedire quam
agrum optime colore*)*

He that tilleth his land
shall have plenty of bread;
But he that followeth after vain
persons shall have poverty enough.

Proverbs 28:19

The early man never borrows
from the late man.

*(timing is the most important factor
in crop production)*

Who soweth too lateward
hath seldom good seed;
Who soweth too soon,
little better shall speed;
Apt time and season,
so diverse to hit;
Let aier and layer
help practice and wit.

Thomas Tusser (1524-80)

We must not spend all the time whetting the scythe.

(preparation is not the same as toil)

He who rides behind another
does not saddle when he pleases.

(the person in front is always in charge)

My father once decided to start harvest on a Friday, and the men went out of Thursday evening, and, unpaid, cut along one side of the first field with their scythes, in order to dodge the malign fate which a Friday start would begin.

A G Street, Remembrances *(1933)*

My one man, my two men,
Will mow me down the medda';
My three men, my four men,
Will carry away togedda';
My five men, my six men,
And there ain't no more,
Will mow my hay, and carry away,
And mow me down the medda'.

old Kentish song

It is better to reap two days too soon than one day too late.

(in farming the weather can make a vast difference to a good or bad harvest)

He that hath a good harvest
may be content with some thistles.

(a variant of 'Every rose has its thorn')

On corner walls, a glittering row,
Hang fire irons — less for use than show;
With horse-shoe brightened, as a spell,
Witchcraft's evil powers to quell.

John Clare, Shepherd's Calendar *(1827)*
(iron was an effective defence against evil)

Blacksmith-made latches on a barn door were often marked with a cross to prevent evil from entering.

(iron was also held to be effective in keeping witches at bay; this traditional mark can still be seen in many parts of the countryside)

To prevent witches, hang a
horse shoe on the inside of
a threshold with three nails.
The heel must be upwards.

Astrological Practice, *1671*

To keep a stable safe from
bewitchment, hang up hooks
and shears. This will scare the
witch who seeks to ride a mare
and leave it with a tangled mane.

Robert Herrick, 1648

Fresh herring plenty Michael brings,
With fatted crones and such old things.

St Michael's Day falls on 29th September,
when tenants also paid their rents;
'crones' were old ewes

Birds & Beasts

Hunting dogs always
have scratched faces.

*(work always exacts a toll
upon the worker)*

Mouse-ear, or Scorpion grass, any
manner of which was ministered
to horses, brings this help unto
them, that they cannot be hurt,
while the smith is shoeing of them,
therefore it is called of many,
herba clavorum, the herb of nails.

traditional, before 1660
(mouse-ear or Myosotis scorpioides *is
now called forget-me-not; the name was
changed in the Victorian period)*

There's aye some water
where the stirkie droons.

*(a 'stirkie' is a bullock or heifer, and young
stock did not understand the dangers of
sudden deep water where unaware
beasts could easily be drowned)*

One swallow proveth not
that summer is near.

1577

If a mule goes wandering
it will not come back a horse.

(there are some things you cannot change)

Fat horses spell foul farms.

(a fat horse is an idle horse)

One white leg — buy a horse;
Two white legs — try a horse;
Three white legs — look well about him;
Four white legs — do without him.

(a supersition that horses with four white legs were to be avoided)

May kittens never make good cats.

A bird in the hand
is worth two flying by.

Scottish version of the
well-known English proverb

One is sorrow, two mirth,
Three for a wedding, four a birth,
Five heaven, six hell,
Seven's the de'il's ain sell.

traditional proverb about magpies

Sheep should never hear the church bells ring twice in the same field.

(sheep fare best on fresh grass)

It's a poor prospect for any parish
when the dogs outnumber the sheep.

When a dog barks
another will join it.

Saints & Seasons

If that Christmas Day should fall
Upon a Friday, know we alle
That winter season shall be easy,
Save great winds aloft shall fly.

If Christmas Day on Monday be,
A great winter that year you'll see.

Saint Mathee
shut up the bee.

Saint Matthew's Day falls on 21st September.

Saint Swithun's Day, if thou dost rain,
For forty days it will remain;
Saint Swithun's Day, if thou be fair,
For forty days 'twill rain na mair.

Scottish rhyme
(St Swithin's Day falls on 15th July)

The Druids cut mistletoe off the trees with their upright hatchets of brass, called *celts*, put upon the ends of their staffs, which they carried in their hands.

William Stukeley (1687-1765), antiquarian, known as the Arch-Druid

Apples, peares, hawthorns, quicksets, oakes.
Sett them at All Hallow-tyde,
and command them to grow;
Sett them at Candlemas-tyde,
and entreat them to grow.

Wiltshire
(All Hallows falls on 1st November and Candlemas on 2nd February; this old saying reminds us of the climatic difference between November and February)

Who knows what I have got
In a hot pot?
Baked Wardens — all hot!
Who knows what I have got?

(the cry of Bedford boys as they carried baked pears about the town on St Simon & St Jude's Day (28th October))

Summer in winter and a summer flood
Never boded England good.

Sow peas and beans
in the wane of the moon.
Who soweth them sooner
he soweth too soon.

(the phases of the moon were
thought to affect a crop's growth)

Who soweth in rain
Hath weed for his pain;
But worse shall he speed
That soweth ill seed.

Thomas Tusser (1524-80)

Barnaby bright, Barnaby bright,
The longest day and the shortest night.

*(The Feast of St Barnabas
falls on 11th June)*

Superstitions

It was said to be safe to shelter under
an elder tree during a thunderstorm
as its wood was used to make the
Cross of Calvary. So the lightning
will never strike an eldern tree.

Chambers Book of Days, *1864*

He that buys land buys many stones,
He that buys flesh buys many bones,
He that buys eggs buys many shells,
He that buys good ale buys nothing else.

March comes in with an adder's head
and goes out with a peacock's tail.

On March the Fourth
the adders come forth.

Isle of Wight

Better to be bitten by a snake
Than to feel the sun in March.

Wiltshire

Spit on a frog's head in March and
the frog will carry your cough away.

North-country old wives' tale

When a toad crosses the road
on a summer afternoon,
rain is at hand.

Fairy loaves were credited with special powers. Possession of one would ensure that the householder would never run out of bread. Cottagers who had a bread oven would place a fairy loaf close to its door to help the bread rise.

Vulgar Errors, *1669*

(fairy loaves = fossilised sea urchins)

You should never pass a black feather
lying on the ground, without sticking
it upright in the soil.

Shropshire, 1883

A drover received his payment from the butcher and returned a small coin as a 'luck-penny'. This determined that he would be likely to return.

Edinburgh Courant, *1805*
(in the days before railways, animals were driven to market along country roads)

God save all here
saving the cat.

Irish blessing on entering a house (cats were excepted on account of their alleged association with witchcraft)

Sailors wives, in Scarborough, often kept a black cat to ensure the safety of their menfolk at sea. In that part of the country it is said that many black cats were stolen by those who also sought protection.

1866

Other books published by Countryman:

The Countryman Companion vol 2
The Countryman Companion vol 3
The Little Book of Yorkshire
The Little Book of Lancashire
The Little Book of the Lake District
The Little Book of Yorkshire Christmas